Julian and Maxie
with

The Perfect Hour

The Perfect Hour

selected poems by Sophia de Mello Breyner Andresen

translated from the Portuguese by

Colin Rorrison with Margaret Jull Costa

Cold Hub Press

First edition

Cold Hub Press
PO Box 156
Lyttelton 8841
New Zealand
coldhubpress.co.nz

ISBN: 978-0-473-31652-5

A catalogue record for this book is available
from the National Library of New Zealand

Cover photograph:
Sophia among fishing nets at Vila Praia de Âncora,
c. 1950, used with permission of the family
of Sophia de Mello Breyner Andresen.

Book design: Roger Hickin
Printed by Toltech Print Ltd, Christchurch, New Zealand

CONTENTS

from *O Nome das Coisas*, 1972-75

from *Dia do Mar*, 1947

Sophia de Mello Breyner Andresen — known simply as Sophia to Portuguese readers — was born in 1919 in Viana do Castelo in the north of Portugal. Brought up in a wealthy Catholic family, she remained true to her faith until her death, although she was also fiercely critical of the repressive right-wing Salazar regime. She married the journalist and lawyer, Francisco Sousa Tavares, by whom she had five children. Introduced by her nanny to the joys of poetry and story-telling, Sophia published her first collection of poems in 1945 and went on to write many further collections, as well as short stories and children's books. She became Portugal's most acclaimed poet. Indeed, she was the first woman to be awarded Portugal's highest literary honour, the Prémio Camões. After the 1974 Carnation Revolution, she was elected as a member of parliament for the Socialist Party.

She is probably the best-known and most loved of Portuguese poets, along with Fernando Pessoa, whose work she admired enormously and who often appears in her poems. Her poetry, however, is very different from his. Her poems show a deep connection with the natural world, her main subjects being childhood and youth, nature and, above all, the sea. She was also steeped in classical literature, and some of her Greek-inspired poems are present in this selection.

I should perhaps say something about the origin of these translations. I met Colin Rorrison when he attended a week-long translation summer school in London in 2011. I was the Portuguese tutor. Colin wrote to me afterwards to ask if I could suggest some Portuguese poets he might translate. I immediately recommended Sophia, and quite unbeknown to me and to his parents, Helen and

Hugh Rorrison, he translated many of the poems that appear in Sophia's two very different collections: *Dia do Mar* and *O Nome das Coisas*. As Helen Rorrison explains in her note [p.101] Colin died tragically young, leaving behind not only his translations of Sophia's poems, but also some excellent translations of various short stories by the Brazilian and Argentinian writers, Rubem Fonseca and Carlos Chernov. Helen and Hugh sent me his Sophia translations, and when I read them, I immediately felt that we should try and find a publisher for them. I also felt that they needed some editing. It seemed to me that these were not final drafts and that we would be doing a disservice to Colin and to Sophia if we tried to publish them as they stood. Also, since what we wanted was a bilingual edition, the poems had to be able to stand up to the implacable scrutiny of the original on the facing page. I drafted and re-drafted, always trying to keep close to Colin's version, but occasionally departing from it quite radically. I then sent my re-drafted versions to Helen and Hugh for their comments (they are also translators — from German). It cannot always have been easy for them to see what I had done. These were Colin's words, after all, and here I was interfering with them. As it turned out, however, it was a labour of love for all three of us. During the summer school where I first met Colin, our small Portuguese group had worked together on translating a very brief poem by Fernando Pessoa. Editing Colin's Sophia translations and comparing notes with Helen and Hugh felt very much like a continuation of that fascinating experience. And when Roger Hickin of Cold Hub Press responded enthusiastically to the translations, this gave wings to our project, which was and is a celebration of Sophia and of Colin.

A brief word about the two collections from which these poems are taken. *Dia do Mar* was published in 1947, when Sophia was 28.

Its subjects are gardens, the sea, the beach and the house, and its central theme, the search for perfection, purity and harmony. The poems have all the intensity of childhood memories, but are imbued, too, with an adult awareness of mortality.

O Nome das Coisas was published thirty years later, in 1977, after the Carnation Revolution of 25th April 1974 and the overthrow of the Salazar/Caetano regime after almost fifty years of repression. As I mentioned earlier, Sophia had been an outspoken critic of the regime and, in these poems, while she embraces the Revolution, she is also critical of the shortcomings of some of the leaders and politicians who came to power in its wake. The political poems refer to a particular time and place and to a particular situation, and yet they remain strikingly bracing and fresh. The poem that begins, 'Nestes últimos tempos'/'Lately' (p. 90) rings particularly true for our own confused times.

I had always loved Sophia's poems, but had, at the same time, felt that her highly personal and often enigmatic brand of poetry might not necessarily translate well into English. I am primarily a translator of prose and although I read a lot of poetry and have dabbled in translating poetry, I have always felt a kind of unease or frustration that I don't feel when translating prose. Perhaps it is the scrutinising gaze of the original telling me that my translation really isn't the same thing at all. And it isn't. It can't be. First of all, Sophia uses rhyme in many of these poems. Colin had opted not to rhyme, which I felt was a very wise decision. It is easy to rhyme in Portuguese, less so in English, and for a translator to maintain rhyme and sense without distorting both is a difficult and not very desirable thing. What we have aimed to do here is to provide translations that clearly reflect the original, so that the reader can look from English to Portuguese and see the connections. What I hope we have achieved is to preserve Sophia's linguistic precision, the right word in the right place and, where possible, with the right sound, although given the different roots and sound systems of the two languages, this has not always been possible.

Perhaps it would be helpful to look at the decisions made in translating just one poem.

Oásis

Penetraremos no palmar
A água será clara o leite doce
O calor será leve o linho branco e fresco
O silêncio estará nu — o canto
Da flauta será nítido no liso
Da penumbra

Lavaremos nossas mãos de desencontro e poeira

Oasis

We will enter the grove of palms
The water will be clear the milk sweet
The air will be balmy the linen white and fresh
The silence will be naked — the song
Of the flute will shine in the softness
Of the half-light

We will wash our hands of disagreement and dust

This is a poem of exquisite simplicity, and I hope that we have managed to reproduce the calm, almost stately rhythm of the original.

As with all of Sophia's poems, the words are chosen with great care. 'O calor será leve' would translate literally as 'The heat will be light/mild/gentle, but in English we have that wonderfully evocative word 'balmy', with all its echoes of 'balmy summer nights'. 'o canto/Da flauta será nítido' means literally: 'the song of the flute will be clear/distinct/bright'. We chose to make the adjective 'nítido' a verb — 'shine', and while in translating 'liso' as 'softness', we have lost the repetition of sounds in the Portuguese ('nítido'/'liso'), we have replaced that with two nicely sussurating words in 'shine' and 'softness'. 'Penumbra' is often a difficult word to translate into English, because although we do, of course, have the word 'penumbra', it can sound too technical and here perhaps too Latinate for such a simple poem. And so we opted for the more Anglo-Saxon 'half-light'. Where Portuguese favours rhyme, English loves alliteration. And in the final line, Colin found a lovely alliterative translation of 'desencontro e poeira' — 'disagreement and dust', which has a satisfyingly conclusive quality, as well as bringing with it all the literary and Biblical echoes of the word 'dust' . That's what happens in translation, you use the riches of your own language to compensate for the inevitable loss of the riches of the original language. That, at least, is the aim.

Margaret Jull Costa

from *Dia do Mar*, 1947

As ondas quebravam uma a uma
Eu estava só com a areia e com a espuma
Do mar que cantava só p'ra mim.

The waves were breaking one by one
I was alone with the sand and with the foam
Of the sea that was singing just for me.

Jardim do mar

Vi um jardim que se desenrolava
Ao longo de uma encosta suspenso
Milagrosamente sobre o mar
Que do largo contra ele cavalgava
Desconhecido e imenso.

Jardim de flores selvagens e duras
E cactos torcidos em mil dobras,
Caminhos de areia branca e estreitos
Entre as rochas escuras
E aqui além, os pinheiros
Magros e direitos.

Jardim do mar, do sol e do vento,
Áspero e salgado,
Pelos duros elementos devastado
Como por um obscuro tormento:
E que não podendo como as ondas
Florescer em espuma,
Raivoso atira para o largo, uma a uma,
As pétalas redondas
Das suas raras flores.

Sea garden

I saw a garden that unfurled itself
Down a steep slope and perched
Miraculously above the sea
Galloping towards it from afar,
Vast and unknown.

Garden of wild unyielding flowers
And cactuses twisted thousand-fold,
Narrow paths of white sand
Among the dark rocks
And further off the pine trees
Thin, erect.

Garden of sea, sun and wind,
Rough and salty,
Eroded by the harsh elements
As if by some obscure torment:
And which unlike the waves
Cannot blossom into foam
But furiously flings down, one by one,
The rounded petals
Of its rare blooms.

Jardim que a água chama e devora
Exausto pelos mil esplendores
De que o mar se reveste em cada hora.

Jardim onde o vento batalha
E que a mão do mar esculpe e talha.
Nu, áspero, devastado,
Numa contínua exaltação,
Jardim quebrado
Da imensidão.
Estreita taça
A transbordar da anunciação
Que às vezes nas coisas passa.

Mar sonoro

Mar sonoro, mar sem fundo, mar sem fim,
A tua beleza aumenta quando estamos sós
E tão fundo intimamente a tua voz
Segue o mais secreto bailar do meu sonho
Que momentos há em que eu suponho
Seres um milagre criado só para mim.

Garden summoned by the waters then devoured
Exhausted by the thousand splendours
With which the sea invests itself hour by hour.

Garden where the wind does battle
Sculpted and shaped by the hand of the sea.
Naked, harsh, battered
In a state of continuous exaltation,
Garden chiselled
Out of the vastness.
Its slender cup
Overflowing with the annunciation
Sometimes granted to mere things.

Sonorous sea

Sonorous, fathomless, endless sea,
When we're alone your beauty grows
And so closely does your voice
Match the most secret dance of my dreams
I imagine sometimes you're
A miracle created just for me.

O jardim

O jardim está brilhante e florido.
Sobre as ervas, entre as folhagens,
O vento passa, sonhador e distraído,
Peregrino de mil romagens.

É Maio ácido e multicolor,
Devorado pelo próprio ardor,
Que nesta clara tarde de cristal
Avança pelos caminhos
Até os fantásticos desalinhos
Do meu bem e do meu mal.

E no seu bailado levada
Pelo jardim deliro e divago,
Ora espreitando debruçada
Os jardins do fundo do lago,
Ora perdendo o meu olhar
Na indizível verdura
Das folhas novas e tenras
Onde eu queria saciar
A minha longa sede de frescura.

The garden

The garden is brilliant and in bloom,
Over the weeds, among the foliage,
The wind passes, dreamy and distracted,
Pilgrim of a thousand pilgrimages.

May, acidic and multicoloured,
Devoured by its own ardour,
Moves on this crystal-clear evening
Along paths that lead
To the fantastical chaos
Of my good and my evil.

And carried by its dance
Through the garden, I drift and dream,
Now leaning over to spy
On the gardens at the bottom of the lake,
Now gazing, lost,
At the indescribable greenness
Of the new and tender leaves
Where I hoped to slake
My long thirst for freshness.

Espera

Dei-te a solidão do dia inteiro.
Na praia deserta, brincando com a areia,
No silêncio que apenas quebrava a maré cheia
A gritar o seu eterno insulto,
Longamente esperei que o teu vulto
Rompesse o nevoeiro.

Esgotei o meu mal

Esgotei o meu mal, agora
Queria tudo esquecer, tudo abandonar
Caminhar pela noite fora
Num barco em pleno mar.

Mergulhar as mãos nas ondas escuras
Até que elas fossem essas mãos
Solitárias e puras
Que eu sonhei ter.

Waiting

I offered you the solitude of a whole day.
On the empty beach, playing in the sand,
In the silence broken only by the rising tide
Calling out its eternal insult,
How I longed for your face
To break through the mist.

With all my evil exhausted

With all my evil exhausted,
I want to forget everything, abandon everything
And set off into the night
On a ship on the open sea.

Plunge my hands into the dark waves
Until they become the hands
Solitary and pure
I always dreamed of having.

É esta a hora...

É esta a hora perfeita em que se cala
O confuso murmurar das gentes
E dentro de nós finalmente fala
A voz grave dos sonhos indolentes.

É esta a hora em que as rosas são as rosas
Que floriram nos jardins persas
Onde Saadi e Hafiz as viram e as amaram.
É esta a hora das vozes misteriosas
Que os meus desejos preferiram e chamaram.
É esta a hora das longas conversas
Das folhas com as folhas unicamente.
É esta a hora em que o tempo é abolido
E nem sequer conheço a minha face.

This is the perfect hour

This is the perfect hour when a hush descends
On our muted human murmurings
And inside us finally there speaks
The grave voice of indolent dreams.

This is the hour when roses are the roses
That flowered in the Persian gardens
Where Saadi and Hafiz saw and loved them.
This is the hour of the mysterious voices
Chosen and summoned by my desires.
This is the hour of the long conversations
Held between leaf and leaf.
This is the hour when time is abolished
And I do not even know my own face.

As rosas

Quando à noite desfolho e trinco as rosas
É como se prendesse entre os meus dentes
Todo o luar das noites transparentes,
Todo o fulgor das tardes luminosas,
O vento bailador das Primaveras,
A doçura amarga dos poentes,
E a exaltação de todas as esperas.

Dia de hoje

Ó dia de hoje, ó dia de horas claras
Florindo nas ondas, cantando nas florestas,
No teu ar brilham transparentes festas
E o fantasma das maravilhas raras
Visita, uma por uma, as tuas horas
Em que há por vezes súbitas demoras
Plenas como as pausas dum verso.

Ó dia de hoje, ó dia de horas leves
Bailando na doçura
E na amargura
De serem perfeitas e de serem breves.

The roses

When at night I strip off the leaves and bite into the stem
It's as if I were grasping between my teeth
All the moonlight of transparent nights,
All the glare of luminous afternoons,
The dancing Spring wind,
The bittersweet sunset,
And the exaltation of all my waitings.

Today

O day today, O day of bright hours
Blooming on the waves, singing in the forests,
The air glitters transparent, caressing,
And the ghost of strange marvels
Visits, one by one, your every hour
Sometimes with sudden rests
As full as the pauses in a line of verse.

O day today, O day of fleeting hours
Dancing in the sweetness
And the bitterness
Of being both perfect and brief.

Abril

Vinhas descendo ao longo das estradas,
Mais leve do que a dança
Como seguindo o sonho que balança
Através das ramagens inspiradas.

E o jardim tremeu,
Pálido de esperança.

Jardim verde

Jardim verde e em flor, jardim de buxo
Onde o poente interminável arde
Enquanto bailam lentas as horas da tarde.
Os narcisos ondulam e o repuxo,
Voz onde o silêncio se embala,
Canta, murmura e fala
Dos paraísos desejados,
Cuja lembrança enche de bailados
A clara solidão das tuas ruas.

April

You came strolling down the street,
Lighter than any dancer
As if following the dream that wafts
Through the wind-inspired branches.

And the garden trembled,
Pale with hope.

Garden green

Garden green and blooming, garden of boxwood
Where the sunset endlessly burns
While the evening hours dance slowly by.
The narcissi sway, and the fountain,
A voice cradling the silence to sleep,
Sings, murmurs and speaks
Of longed-for paradises,
The remembrance of which fills with dancing
The bright solitude of your paths.

Promessa

És tu a Primavera que eu esperava,
A vida multiplicada e brilhante,
Em que é pleno e perfeito cada instante.

Dionysos

Entre as árvores escuras e caladas
O céu vermelho arde,
E nascido da secreta cor da tarde
Dionysos passa na poeira das estradas.

A abundância dos frutos de Setembro
Habita a sua face e cada membro
Tem essa perfeiçao vermelha e plena,
Essa glória ardente e serena
Que distinguia os deuses dos mortais.

Promise

It's you, Spring, I was waiting for,
Life multiplied and brilliant,
In which every instant is perfect and complete.

Dionysus

Among the dark and silent trees
The crimson sky burns,
And born of the secret colour of the evening
Dionysus moves through the dusty streets.

The abundance of September fruits
Fills his face, and every limb
Has that same full crimson perfection,
The same serene, ardent glory
That once distinguished the gods from mortals.

Os deuses

Nasceram, como um fruto, da paisagem.
A brisa dos jardins, a luz do mar,
O branco das espumas e o luar
Extasiados estão na sua imagem.

O anjo

O Anjo que em meu redor passa e me espia
E cruel me combate, nesse dia
Veio sentar-se ao lado do meu leito
E embalou-me, cantando, no seu peito.

Ele que indiferente olha e me escuta
Sofrer, ou que, feroz comigo luta,
Ele que me entregara à solidão,
Poisava a sua mão na minha mão.

E foi como se tudo se extinguisse.
Como se o mundo inteiro se calasse,
E o meu ser liberto enfim florisse,
E um perfeito silêncio me embalasse.

The gods

They were born, like fruit, from the land.
The breeze from the gardens, the light from the sea,
The white foam and the moonlight
Stand ecstatic and amazed in their image.

The angel

The angel who stalks and watches me
And cruelly fights with me, on that day
Came to sit by my bed
Held me to his breast and sang me to sleep.

The angel who, indifferent, watches and hears
Me suffer or grapples with me,
Who had surrendered me to solitude,
Was placing his hand on my hand.

And it was as if everything stopped,
As if the whole world fell silent,
And my liberated self finally flowered,
And a perfect silence rocked me to sleep.

Gruta de Camões

Dentro de mim sobe a imagem dessa gruta
Cujo silêncio ainda escuta
Os teus gestos e os teus passos.

Aí, diante do mar como tu transbordante
De confissão e segredo,
Choraste a face pura
Das brancas amadas
Mortas tão cedo.

*Camões' Grotto**

Inside me rises the image of that grotto
Whose silence can still hear
Your gestures and your footsteps.

There, before the sea overflowing like you
With confessions and secrets,
You wept for the pure faces
Of your pale lady loves
Dead all too soon.

Camões' Grotto is reputedly the former home of Portugal's national poet,
Luís de Camões, when he lived in Macau (then a Portuguese colony).
He is said to have written his great epic *The Lusiads* there.

Navio naufragado

Vinha dum mundo
Sonoro, nítido e denso.
E agora o mar o guarda no seu fundo
Silencioso e suspenso.

É um esqueleto branco o capitão,
Branco como as areias,
Tem duas conchas na mão
Tem algas em vez de veias
E uma medusa em vez de coração.

Em seu redor as grutas de mil cores
Tomam formas incertas quase ausentes
E a cor das águas toma a cor das flores
E os animais são mudos, transparentes.

E os corpos espalhados nas areias
Tremem à passagem das sereias,
As sereias leves dos cabelos roxos
Que têm olhos vagos e ausentes
E verdes como os olhos dos videntes.

Shipwreck

It came from a world
Sonorous, brilliant, dense,
And now the sea keeps it in its depths,
Suspended and silent.

The captain is a white skeleton,
White as the sands,
He holds two shells in his hand
He has seaweed for veins
And a jellyfish in place of a heart.

Around him the caves of many colours
Take on vague, evanescent shapes
And the water takes on the colour of flowers,
And every creature is dumb, transparent.

And the bodies scattered on the sands
Tremble as the mermaids pass,
Weightless mermaids with purple hair
With distant, absent eyes
Green as the eyes of visionaries.

Goyesca

Um infinito ardor
Quase triste os veste,
Semelhante ao sabor
Que tem à noite o vento leste.

Bailam na doçura amarga
Da tarde brilhante e densa
E cada gesto que se alarga
Tem a morte em si suspensa.

Goyesca

An infinite, almost sad ardour
Clothes them, tastes like
The east wind at night.

They dance in the bittersweetness
Of this dense and dazzling afternoon
And every gesture extended
Contains death suspended.

Estranha noite

Estranha noite velada,
Sem estrelas e sem lua,
Em cuja bruma recua
Fantasma de si mesma cada imagem.

Jaz em ruínas a paisagem,
A dissolução habita cada linha.
Enorme, lenta e vaga
A noite ferozmente apaga
Tudo quanto eu era e quanto eu tinha.

E mais silenciosa do que um lago,
Sobre a agonia desse mundo vago,
A morte dança
E em seu redor tudo recua
Sem força e sem esperança.

Tudo o que era certo se dissolve;
O mar e a praia tudo se resolve
Na mesma solidão eterna e nua.

Strange veiled night

Strange veiled night
With no stars no moon,
Into whose mists every image
Retreats like a ghost of itself.

The landscape lies in ruins,
Dissolution inhabits every line.
Vast, slow and empty
The night ferociously extinguishes
Everything I was and everything I had.

And more silent than a lake,
Above the agony of this empty world,
Death dances
And all around everything recedes
Drained of strength and hope.

All certainty dissolves;
The sea and beach, everything resolves itself
Into the same eternal, naked solitude.

Sonhei com lúcidos delírios

Sonhei com lúcidos delírios
À luz de um puro amanhecer
Numa planície onde crescem lírios
E há regatos cantantes a correr.

Quem como eu

Quem como eu em silêncio tece
Bailados, jardins e harmonias?
Quem como eu se perde e se dispersa
Nas coisas e nos dias?

I dreamed in lucid delirium

I dreamed in lucid delirium
Of the light of a pure dawn
On a plain where lilies grow
And streams sing as they flow.

Who like me

Who like me in the silence weaves
Dances and gardens and harmonies?
Who like me is lost and dispersed
In things and in days?

Lua

Entre a terra e os astros, flor intensa,
Nascida do silêncio, a lua cheia
Dá vertigens ao mar e azula a areia,
E a terra segue-a em êxtases suspensa.

Dança de Junho

Em silêncio nas coisas embaladas
Vão dançando ao sabor dos seus segredos.
Nos seus vestidos brancos e bordados
Raios de lua poisam como dedos,
E em seu redor baloiçam arvoredos
Escuros entre os céus atormentados.

Moon

Between earth and stars, an intense flower,
Born of the silence, the full moon
Makes the sea giddy and the sand blue,
And the earth follows her, rapt, ecstatic.

June dance

In silence lulled and rocked
They dance to the rhythm of their secrets.
On their white embroidered clothes
Moonbeams rest like fingers,
And around them sway treetops
Dark among the tormented skies.

Um dia

Um dia, mortos, gastos, voltaremos
A viver livres como os animais
E mesmo tão cansados floriremos
Irmãos vivos do mar e dos pinhais.

O vento levará os mil cansaços
Dos gestos agitados, irreais,
E há-de voltar aos nossos membros lassos
A leve rapidez dos animais.

Só então poderemos caminhar
Através do mistério que se embala
No verde dos pinhais, na voz do mar
E em nós germinará a sua fala.

One day

One day, though dead and spent, we will return
To live free as the animals
And however weary we will flourish,
The living brothers of the sea and the pines.

The wind will sweep away all tiredness
In our agitated, unreal gestures,
And to our weary legs will be restored
The light swiftness of animals.

Only then will we be able to walk
Through the mystery that lies cradled
In the green of the pines, in the voice of the sea,
And in us its language will set seed.

Evadir-me, esquecer-me

Evadir-me, esquecer-me, regressar
À frescura das coisas vegetais,
Ao verde flutuante dos pinhais
Percorridos de seivas virginais
E ao grande vento límpido do mar.

As imagens transbordam

As imagens transbordam fugitivas
E estamos nus em frente às coisas vivas.
Que presença jamais pode cumprir
O impulso que há em nós, interminável,
De tudo ser e em cada flor florir?

To escape, to forget

To escape, to forget, to return
To the freshness of growing things,
To the fluctuating green of the pines
Filled with virgin sap
And to the great clear wind of the sea.

The fugitive images overflow

The fugitive images overflow
And we stand naked before all living things.
What presence could ever satisfy
That never-ending impulse to be everything,
And in every flower to bloom?

Noite

Noite de folha em folha murmurada,
Branca de mil silêncios, negra de astros,
Com desertos de sombra e luar, dança
Imperceptível em gestos quietos.

Divaga entre a folhagem

Divaga entre a folhagem perfumada
E adormece nas brisas embalada.

Aos lagos mostra a sua face nua,
E vai dançar nos palcos vazios da Lua.

Pálida, de reflexo em reflexo desliza,
Não se curvam sequer as ervas que ela pisa.

É ela quem baloiça os lânguidos pinheiros,
Quem enrola em luar as suas mãos
E depois as espalha brancas nos canteiros.

Night

Night murmured from leaf to leaf,
White with a thousand silences, black with stars,
Among deserts of shadow and moonlight it dances
An almost imperceptible dance.

She wanders among the perfumed foliage

She wanders among the perfumed foliage
And falls asleep lulled by the breeze.

To the lakes she displays her naked face,
And slips away to dance on the Moon's bare stage.

Pale, from reflection to reflection she glides,
Not even the grass bends beneath her feet.

It is she who sways the languid pine trees,
She who wraps her hands in moonlight
And scatters their whiteness among the flowerbeds.

Floresta

Entre o terror e a noite caminhei
Não em redor das coisas mas subindo
Através do calor das suas veias
Não em redor das coisas mas morrendo
Transfigurada em tudo quanto amei.

Entre o luar e a sombra caminhei:
Era ali a minha alma, cada flor
— Cega, secreta e doce como estrelas —
Quando a tocava nela me tornei.

E as árvores abriram os seus ramos
Os seus ramos enormes e convexos
E no estranho brilhar dos seus reflexos
Oscilavam sinais, quebrados ecos
Que no silêncio fantástico beijei.

Forest

Between terror and the night I walked
Not around things but ascending
Through the heat of their veins
Not around things but dying
Transfigured into all that I loved.

Between moonlight and the shadows I walked:
There lay my soul, and with each flower
— Blind, secret and sweet as stars —
Just one touch and I became that flower.

And the trees opened their branches
Their branches vast and convex
And in the strange glow of their reflections
Glimmered messages and broken echoes
Which in the fantastic silence I embraced.

Se alguém passa

Se alguém passa agora nos areais,
Se alguém passa agora nos pinhais,
Diz,
Em gestos plenos e naturais,
Tudo o que eu, tão em vão, perdidamente quis.

Há jardins

Há jardins invadidos de luar
Que vibram no silêncio como liras.
Segura o teu amor entre os teus dedos
Neste jardim de Abril em que respiras.

A vida não virá — as tuas mãos
Não podem colher noutras a doçura
Das flores baloiçando ao vento leve.

Fosse o teu corpo feito de luar,
Fosses tu o jardim cheio de lagos,
As árvores em flor, a profusão
Da sua sombra negra nos caminhos.

Anyone walking

Anyone walking across the sands now,
Anyone walking through the pinewoods now,
Is saying,
In generous, natural gestures,
Everything that I, so desperately, vainly, wanted to say.

There are gardens

There are gardens invaded by moonlight
That vibrate in the silence like lyres.
Hold fast to the love between your fingers
In this April garden in which you breathe.

Life will not come — your hands
Cannot pick with any other hands the sweetness
Of the flowers swaying in the gentle wind.

Not even if your body were made of moonlight,
Not even if you were the garden filled with lakes,
The blossoming trees, the profusion
Of their dark shadows along the paths.

from *O Nome das Coisas,* 1972-75

Che Guevara

Contra ti se ergueu a prudência dos inteligentes e o arrojo
                                    [dos patetas
A indecisão dos complicados e o primarismo
Daqueles que confundem revolução com desforra

De poster em poster a tua imagem paira na sociedade de
                                    [consumo
Como o Cristo em sangue paira no alheamento ordenado das
                                    [igrejas

Porém
Em frente do teu rosto
Medita o adolescente à noite no seu quarto
Quando procura emergir de um mundo que apodrece

Lisboa, 1972

Che Guevara

Against you stood the prudence of the intelligent and the
                                                [boldness of fools
The indecision of the complicators and the primitivism
Of those who confuse revolution with revenge

From poster to poster your image haunts our consumer
                                                [society
As the bleeding Christ haunts the orderly alienation of the
                                                [church

And yet
Before your face
The adolescent in his room at night meditates
As he strives to emerge from a world in decay

Lisbon, 1972

Guerra ou Lisboa 72

Partiu vivo jovem forte
Voltou bem grave e calado
Com morte no passaporte

Sua morte nos jornais
Surgiu em letra pequena
É preciso que o país
Tenha a consciência serena

Como o rumor

Como o rumor do mar dentro de um búzio
O divino sussurra no universo
Algo emerge: primordial projecto

War or Lisbon 1972

He left young strong and alive
He came back solemn and silent
With death on his passport

His death in the newspapers
Appeared in small print
The country needs
An untroubled conscience

Like the murmur

Like the murmur of the sea inside a shell
The divine whispers through the universe
Something emerges: a primordial plan

Sua beleza

Sua beleza é total
Tem a nítida esquadria de um Mantegna
Porém como um Picasso de repente
Desloca o visual

Seu torso lembra o respirar da vela
Seu corpo é solar e frontal
Sua beleza à força de ser bela
Promete mais do que prazer
Promete um mundo mais inteiro e mais real
Como pátria do ser

'Fernando Pessoa' ou 'Poeta em Lisboa'

Em sinal de sorte ou desgraça
A tua sombra cruza o ângulo da praça
(Trémula incerta impossessiva alheia
E como escrita de lápis leve e baça)
E sob o voo das gaivotas passa
Atropelada por tudo quanto passa

Em sinal de sorte ou de desgraça

Lisboa , 1972

Her beauty

Her beauty is complete
It has the sharp contours of a Mantegna
Yet like a Picasso suddenly
The vision fractures

Her torso recalls the breathing of the candle
Her body is sunny and open
Her beauty as sheer beauty
Promises more than pleasure
Promises a more complete, more real world
A home for humanity

'Fernando Pessoa' or 'Poet in Lisbon'

As a symbol of luck or misfortune
Your shadow crosses the corner of the square
(Tremulous uncertain impossessive other
As though written with a soft blunt pencil)
And you pass beneath the circling seagulls
Jostled by everything else that passes

As a symbol of luck or misfortune

Lisbon, 1972

65

O Palácio

Era um dos palácios do Minotauro
— O da minha infância para mim o primeiro —
Tinha sido construído no século passado (e pintado a vermelho)

Estátuas escadas veludo granito
Tílias o cercavam de música e murmúrio
Paixões e traições o inchavam de grito

Espelhos ante espelhos tudo aprofundavam
Seu pátio era interior era átrio
As suas varandas eram por dentro
Viradas para o centro
Em grandes vazios as vozes ecoavam
Era um dos palácios do Minotauro
O da minha infancia — para mim o vermelho

Ali a magia como fogo ardia de Março a Fevereiro
A prata brilhava o vidro luzia
Tudo tilintava tudo estremecia
De noite e de dia

Era um dos palácios do Minotauro
— O da minha infância para mim o primeiro —
Ali o tumulto cego confundia
O escuro da noite e o brilho do dia
Ali era a fúria o clamor o não-dito
Ali o confuso onde tudo irrompia
Ali era o Kaos onde tudo nascia

The Palace

It was one of the Minotaur's palaces
— The one from my childhood, my first —
Built in the last century (and painted red)

Statues staircases velvet granite
Lime trees surrounded it with music and murmuring
Passions and betrayals filled it with noise

Mirrors upon mirrors made everything deeper
The courtyard was inside not out, an atrium,
Its verandas were inside too
Turned to face the centre
The great void echoing with voices
It was one of the Minotaur's palaces
The one from my childhood — bright red

There from March to February magic burned like fire
The silver shone the glass glistened
Everything tinkled everything trembled
All night all day

It was one of the Minotaur's palaces
— The one from my childhood, my first —
There the blind tumult confounded
Dark night and bright day
There all was fury clamour words unspoken
There the confusion from which all things erupted
There the Chaos from which all things were born

25 de Abril

Esta é a madrugada que eu esperava
O dia inicial inteiro e limpo
Onde emergimos da noite e do silêncio
E livres habitamos a substância do tempo

Revolução

Como casa limpa
Como chão varrido
Como porta aberta

Como puro início
Como tempo novo
Sem mancha nem vício

Como a voz do mar
Interior de um povo

Como página em branco
Onde o poema emerge

Como arquitectura
Do homem que ergue
Sua habitação

27 de Abril de 1974

25th April

This is the day I've been waiting for
The first day whole and clean
Where we emerge from the night and the silence
And freely inhabit the substance of time

Revolution

Like a clean house
Like a swept floor
Like an open door

Like a new beginning
Like time untainted
By stain or defect

Like the voice of the sea
The people's unconscious

Like a blank page
Where a poem emerges

Like the architecture
Of a man who builds
His own dwelling place

27 April 1974

Com fúria e raiva

Com fúria e raiva acuso o demagogo
E o seu capitalismo das palavras

Pois é preciso saber que a palavra é sagrada
Que de longe muito longe um povo a trouxe
E nela pôs sua alma confiada

De longe muito longe desde o início
O homem soube de si pela palavra
E nomeou a pedra a flor a água
E tudo emergiu porque ele disse

Com fúria e raiva acuso o demagogo
Que se promove à sombra da palavra
E da palavra faz poder e jogo
E transforma as palavras em moeda
Como se fez com o trigo e com a terra

Junho de 1974

With furious rage

With furious rage I accuse the demagogue
And his capitalism of words

For it should be known that the word is sacred
That from far far away a people have brought it
And placed in it their trusting soul
From far far away since the beginning
Man knew himself through words
And named the stone the flower the water
And everything emerged because he spoke

With furious rage I accuse the demagogue
Who puffs himself up with the aid of words
And out of words makes power and pastime
And as he did with the wheat and the land
He transforms words into money.

June, 1974

Liberdade

O poema é
A liberdade

Um poema não se programa
Porém a disciplina
— Sílaba por sílaba —
O acompanha

Sílaba por sílaba
O poema emerge
— Como se os deuses o dessem
O fazemos

Retrato de mulher

Algo de cereal e de campestre
Algo de simples em sua claridade
Algo sorri em sua austeridade

Freedom

The poem is
Freedom

A poem doesn't plan itself
But discipline
— Syllable by syllable —
Accompanies it

Syllable by syllable
The poem emerges
— And we create it
As if it were a gift from the gods

Portrait of a woman

Something of corn and the country
Something simple in her clarity
Something smiles in her austerity

Esteira e cesto

No entrançar de cestos ou de esteira
Há um saber que vive e não desterra
Como se o tecedor a si próprio se tecesse
E não entrançasse unicamente esteira e cesto

Mas seu humano casamento com a terra

O Rei de Ítaca

A civilização em que estamos é tão errada que
Nela o pensamento se desligou da mão

Ulisses rei de Ítaca carpinteirou seu barco
E gabava-se também de saber conduzir
Num campo a direito o sulco do arado

Basket and mat

In the weave of baskets and mats
There's a living knowledge that resists exile
As if the weaver wove himself
And not just baskets and mats

But the marriage of man with earth

The King of Ithaca

The civilisation we live in has gone so far astray
Thought has become disconnected from hand

Ulysses King of Ithaca built his own boat
And boasted too that he could plough
A straight furrow in a field

Os erros

A confusão a fraude os erros cometidos
A transparência perdida — o grito
Que não conseguiu atravessar o opaco
O limiar e o linear perdidos

Deverá tudo passar a ser passado
Como projecto falhado e abandonado
Como papel que se atira ao cesto
Como abismo fracasso não esperança
Ou poderemos enfrentar e superar
Recomeçar a partir da página em branco
Como escrita de poema obstinado?

1975

Mistakes

Confusion deceit mistakes made
All transparency lost — the cry
That cannot penetrate the opaque
The liminal the linear quite lost

Must everything become the past
Like a project failed and abandoned
Like a scrap of paper thrown away
Like an abysmal hopeless failure
Or will we confront and overcome
Begin again on a blank page
As if writing a recalcitrant poem?

1975

Caderno I

Quando me perco de novo neste antigo
Caderno de capa preta de oleado —
Que um dia rasguei com fúria e que um amigo
Folha a folha recolou com vagar e paciência —

Tudo me dói ainda como faca e me corta
Pois diante de mim estão como sussurro e floresta
As longas tardes as misturadas noites
Onde divago e divagam incessantemente
Os venenosos perfumes mortais da juventude

E dói-me a luz como um jardim perdido

Notebook I

When I lose myself once again in this old
Notebook with its black oilcloth cover —
Which one day I tore up in fury and which a friend
Slowly patiently page by page glued together again —

Everything still hurts like a knife cutting
Because there before me like a whisper like a forest
Lie the long evenings the jumbled nights
Where I wander and where also ceaselessly wander
The poisonous mortal perfumes of youth

And where the light pains me like a lost garden

Caderno II

Quando me perco de novo neste antigo
Caderno de capa preta de oleado
Que um dia rasguei com fúria e desespero
E que um amigo recolou com amor e paciência

De novo se ergue em minha frente a clara
Parede cal do quarto matinal
Virado para o mar e onde o poente
Se afogueava denso e transparente
E a sonâmbula noite se azulava

Ali o tempo vivido foi tão vivo
Que sempre à própria morte sobrevive
E cada dia julgo que regressa
Seu esplendor de fruto e de promessa

Notebook II

When I lose myself once again in this old
Notebook with its black oilcloth cover
Which one day I tore up in fury and despair
And which a friend glued together lovingly patiently

Once again before me rises the bright
Whitewashed wall of the morning room
Turned towards the sea where the sunset
Was drowning dense and transparent
And the somnambulist night was turning blue

There the time lived was so alive
That it survives even death itself
And every day I believe in its return
In all its glorious fruitful promise

Dia

Mergulho no dia como em mar ou seda
Dia passado comigo e com a casa
Perpassa pelo ar um gesto de asa
Apesar de tanta dor e tanta perda

O Minotauro

Assim o Minotauro longo tempo latente
De repente salta sobre a nossa vida
Com veemência vital de monstro insaciado

Day

I plunge into the day as if into sea or silk
A day spent with myself and at home
A day that glides through the air like a wing
Despite so much pain so much loss

The Minotaur

And so the long-hidden Minotaur
Suddenly pounces on our lives
With the vital energy of an unsated monster

A paixão nua

A paixão nua e cega dos estios
Atravessou a minha vida como rios

Exílio

Exilámos os deuses e fomos
Exilados da nossa inteireza

Oásis

Penetraremos no palmar
A água será clara o leite doce
O calor será leve o linho branco e fresco
O silêncio estará nu — o canto
Da flauta será nítido no liso
Da penumbra

Lavaremos nossas mãos de desencontro e poeira

The blind naked passion

The blind naked passion of summers
Coursed through my life like rivers

Exile

We exiled the gods and were
Exiled from our own completeness

Oasis

We will enter the grove of palms
The water will be clear the milk sweet
The air will be balmy the linen white and fresh
The silence will be naked — the song
Of the flute will shine in the softness
Of the half-light

We will wash our hands of disagreement and dust

Regressarei

Eu regressarei ao poema como à pátria à casa
Como àntiga infância que perdi por descuido
Para buscar obstinada a substância de tudo
E gritar de paixão sob mil luzes acesas

Será possível

Será possível que nada se cumprisse?
Que o roseiral a brisa as folhas de hera
Fossem como palavras sem sentido
— Que nada sejam senão seu rosto ido
Sem regresso nem resposta — só perdido?

I will return

I will return to the poem as though to my country my home
As though to the distant childhood I so carelessly lost
To seek stubbornly for the substance of all things
And cry out with passion beneath a thousand burning lights

Is it possible

Is it possible that nothing happened?
That the rose garden the breeze the ivy leaves
Were just meaningless words
— That they were nothing but your vanished face
With no possible return or response — simply lost?

A Forma Justa

Sei que seria possível construir o mundo justo
As cidades poderiam ser claras e lavadas
Pelo canto dos espaços e das fontes
O céu o mar e a terra estão prontos
A saciar a nossa fome do terrestre
A terra onde estamos — se ninguém atraiçoasse — proporia
Cada dia a cada um a liberdade e o reino
— Na concha na flor no homem e no fruto
Se nada adoecer a própria forma é justa
E no todo se integra como palavra em verso
Sei que seria possível construir a forma justa
De uma cidade humana que fosse
Fiel à perfeição do universo

Por isso recomeço sem cessar a partir da página em branco
E este é meu ofício de poeta para a reconstrução do mundo

The Just Form

I know it must be possible to build a just world
Cities could be bright and washed clean
By the song of open spaces and fountains
Sky sea and earth are ready
To satisfy our hunger for the earthly
And the earth where we are — were there no betrayals — would offer
To everyone every day liberty and the kingdom
— In the shell in the flower in man and in the fruit —
If nothing sickens the form itself is just
Becomes part of the whole like word and verse
I know it must be possible to build the just form
Of a human city
True to the perfection of the universe

That's why I start over and again with a blank page
This is my task as a poet to rebuild the world

Nestes últimos tempos

Nestes últimos tempos é certo a esquerda fez erros
Caiu em desmandos confusões praticou injustiças

Mas que diremos da longa tenebrosa e perita
Degradação das coisas que a direita pratica?

Que diremos do lixo do seu luxo — de seu
Viscoso gozo da nata da vida — que diremos
De sua feroz ganância e fria possessão?

Que diremos de sua sábia e tácita injustiça
Que diremos de seus conluios e negócios
E do utilitário uso dos seus ócios?

Que diremos de suas máscaras álibis e pretextos
De suas fintas labirintos e contextos?

Nestes últimos tempos é certo a esquerda muita vez
Desfigurou as linhas do seu rosto

Mas que diremos da meticulosa eficaz expedita
Degradação da vida que a direita pratica?

Julho de 1976

Lately

Lately it's true the Left have made mistakes
Fallen into rebellions confusions injustices

But what about the long dark devious
Degradation practised by the Right?

What about their trashy treasure — their
Cruel delight in the good things of life — what about
Their ferocious greed and cold possessiveness?

What about their wise and witting injustices
What about their collusions and connivings
Their self-seeking use of even their idle hours?

What about their masks alibis and pretexts
Their feints labyrinths and contexts?

Lately it's true the Left has often
Disfigured its own face

But what about the meticulous competent efficient
Degradation of life practised by the Right?

July 1976

Por delicadeza

Bailarina fui
Mas nunca dancei
Em frente das grades
Só três passos dei

Tão breve o começo
Tão cedo negado
Dancei no avesso
Do tempo bailado

Dançarina fui
Mas nunca bailei
Deixei-me ficar
Na prisão do rei

Onde o mar aberto
E o tempo lavado?
Perdi-me tão perto
Do jardim buscado

Bailarina fui
Mas nunca bailei
Minha vida toda
Como cega errei

Delicatesse

A ballerina was I
But I never danced
Outside the prison bars
I took just three steps

The beginning so brief
So quickly denied
I danced on the other side
Of danced time

A dancer was I
But I never danced
No I stayed safe inside
The king's prison

Where is the open sea
And washed-away time?
I got lost when so very close
To the longed-for garden

A ballerina was I
But I never danced
Spent my whole life
Wandering as though blind

Minha vida atada
Nunca a desatei
Como Rimbaud disse
Também eu direi:

«Juventude ociosa
Por tudo iludida
Por delicadeza
Perdi minha vida»

My life bound by knots
I never untied
As Rimbaud said
So too say I:

'Idle youth
Slave to everything
Out of delicatesse
I have wasted my life'

from *Dia do Mar,* 1947

Quando

Quando o meu corpo apodrecer e eu for morta
Continuará o jardim, o céu e o mar,
E como hoje igualmente hão-de bailar
As quatro estações à minha porta.

Outros em Abril passarão no pomar
Em que eu tantas vezes passei,
Haverá longos poentes sobre o mar,
Outros amarão as coisas que eu amei.

Será o mesmo brilho a mesma festa,
Será o mesmo jardim à minha porta,
E os cabelos doirados da floresta,
Como se eu não estivesse morta.

When

When my body falls sick and I die
The garden will still be here, the sea and the sky,
And the four seasons, just as they do today,
Will dance at my door.

In April, others will stroll in the orchard
Where I so often walked,
There will be long sunsets over the sea,
Others will love the things I loved.

The same glow, the same celebration,
The same garden at my door,
The same golden-haired forest,
Just as if I hadn't died.

This book came into being as a result of the enthusiasm, encouragement and active collaborative work of Margaret Jull Costa. In consultation with Colin Rorrison's parents, a selection was made of some 69 poems from two volumes of Sophia de Mello Breyner Andresen's poetical works (*Obra Poética*). Before he died, Colin had done the groundwork on the translations, and the amount of work he had devoted to these in the months that remained to him is remarkable, particularly as he also produced translations of short prose by a range of writers as diverse as Rubem Fonseca, Carlos Chernov and Cristina Peri Rossi in the same period. It would perhaps be true to say that, in his last months, translation was at the core of Colin's life and this volume is a tribute to that as it is to the work of a poet, who was also a translator. Sophia herself published Portuguese translations of Dante and Shakespeare.

We, as Colin's parents, are immensely grateful to Margaret Jull Costa for taking up this work in progress and finishing what he began. The collection concludes with her translation of the poem 'Quando'/ 'When'.

Helen Rorrison

Colin Rorrison was born in Leeds in 1983 and died suddenly on 8th September 2012, at age 28, in Lomas de Zamora, Buenos Aires Province on his first visit to Latin America. He studied Spanish and Portuguese at the University of Edinburgh and also attended university and college in Coimbra in Portugal and in Málaga and Barcelona in Spain. He was widely read in Iberian and Latin American literature and had translated the text of a new film by Bráulio Mantovani, who wrote the screenplay of *City of God* (*Cidade de Deus,* 2002). He left behind a substantial body of poetry and prose translations from the Portuguese and Spanish, some of which have been published posthumously. His translations of Rubem Fonseca's stories *The Lonely Hearts* and *The Performance* have appeared in the literary magazine, *Hayden's Ferry Review* (2013, 2014) in Arizona. The first was nominated for a Pushcart Prize. His interest in and gift for translation were unlocked at a summer course at London University in 2011. The tutor for Portuguese was Margaret Jull Costa. Colin contacted her afterwards to ask for suggestions of possible poets so that he could enter the annual Stephen Spender Prize competition for poetry in translation in 2012. He went on to translate about 80 poems by Sophia from which he selected three: 'The Garden', 'Shipwreck' and 'The Just Form' for submission. They appear in this volume. The last two were read at his funeral on 20th October, 2012, the first as a poem about death and transfiguration and the second as reflecting the translator's strong sense of the need for justice and humanity in the world, something he shared with the poet.

Margaret Jull Costa has been a literary translator for nearly thirty years and has translated novels and short stories by such writers as Eça de Queiroz, Fernando Pessoa, José Saramago, Javier Marías and Bernardo Atxaga. She has won various prizes, including, in 2008, the PEN/Book-of-the-Month Club Prize and the Oxford Weidenfeld Translation Prize for *The Maias* by Eça de Queiroz, and, most recently, the 2012 Calouste Gulbenkian Translation Prize for *The Word Tree* by Teolinda Gersão, for which she was also runner-up with her translation of António Lobo Antunes' *The Land at the End of the World* (*Os cus de Judas*). In 2013 she was invited to become a Fellow of the Royal Society of Literature and in 2014 was awarded an OBE for services to literature.